HOW TO B(

NETWORK MARKETING BUSINESS IN

15

MINUTES A DAY

KEITH & TOM "BIG AL" SCHREITER

How to Build Your Network Marketing Business
in 15 Minutes a Day

Published by Fortune Network Publishing
PO Box 890084
Houston, TX 77289 USA

Telephone: +1 (281) 280-9800

BigAlBooks.com

ISBN-10: 1-948197-12-X
ISBN-13: 978-1-948197-12-0

CONTENTS

PREFACE

The Pareto principle says that 20% of our work gets 80% of our results. So, why not concentrate on making our 20% the best we can?

What will happen if we only work on the highly-productive 20% that gets the best results? If that happens, we will achieve a lot in a small amount of time.

Would some details and tasks fall through the cracks? Certainly. But if we can live with 80% of the results for now, we can catch up on all the details later.

In this book, we will look at the most important business-building tasks that we can do in the minimum amount of time. Let's get started.

—Keith and Tom "Big Al" Schreiter

I travel the world 240+ days each year.
Let me know if you want me to stop in your
area and conduct a live Big Al training.

→ **BigAlSeminars.com** ←

FREE Big Al Training Audios

Magic Words for Prospecting

plus Free eBook and the Big Al Report!

→ BigAlBooks.com/free ←

15 MINUTES A DAY.

Build a network marketing business in only 15 minutes a day? Is that possible?

15 minutes a day is not ideal. We would love to have more time.

But, if we are a busy parent, overworked, or have severe time restraints, this shouldn't exclude us from the benefits of network marketing.

Everyone should have an opportunity to build a network marketing business, no matter how limited their resources. Let's look at some of the challenges we could have while building our business:

- We have no time.
- We don't know anyone.
- We don't know how to engage people.
- We live in a remote area.
- We have poor social skills.
- We haven't learned network marketing skills yet.
- We are not organized.

Limited time is only one of the many possible challenges we could have.

We can accept the time challenge, move forward and build our businesses. Or, we can let the time challenge defeat us. If we have read this far, we have already made up our minds to defeat our time challenges and move forward.

Our limited time challenges.

It takes focused, concentrated action to build a business in only 15 minutes a day. We need to use this time for prospecting, developing new contacts, presentations, follow-up, coaching, and leading our team. That is a lot to do in 15 minutes.

We can't spend this time shuffling papers or staring out the window while we make plans for next week. These 15 minutes have to be our most productive minutes of the day.

If we focus these minutes on income-producing activities, yes, we can build our business. We will be able to invest more time later.

Even if we are working three jobs, are busy with our family, and have a diary full of obligations, we can participate and build our network marketing business. It won't be as easy as if we had 20 hours a week. But, it is possible.

Do we have 15 minutes a day? Yes. Everyone has 24 hours a day. The richest person in the world and the most care-free slacker ... both have 24 hours a day.

The secret is how we allocate that time.

We can choose what we want to do with our 24 hours. We chose to spend time on a job. We chose to spend time eating and sleeping. Yes, we have the power to set aside 15 minutes for our business.

Even if we feel too busy, we can find 15 minutes in our packed schedules. So, let's get ready to focus. With only 15 minutes a day, we have to be quick and efficient.

Still unsure of what we can accomplish in 15 minutes?

Here is an example of laser-focused achievement in only 15 minutes.

Have we ever received a call from a friend who happens to be close by and wants to stop by for a visit? We hang up the phone, look around the house, and see a disaster zone. The kitchen is full of dishes, laundry piles are everywhere, and the kids' toys are covering every bit of floor space. So what do we do?

We start cleaning like we've never cleaned before. We focus on the task, and in a few short minutes we make our house presentable just as the doorbell rings. It is amazing how much we can do with the proper motivation.

Our 15 minutes a day accumulates over time.

Consistency over time can create huge results. A little bit each day is better than trying to do massive campaigns every few months. Think of our 15 minutes a day as if we were getting in shape. Which method do you think would get the best results?

A. Doing as much as we can for 48 hours until we are exhausted. Then repeat again in a month or two.

B. Exercising regularly for 15 minutes a day.

Obviously, "B" is the better choice. Consistency helps us build habits. And habits don't need constant willpower. This is a better path to success.

The secret is to **schedule** our 15 minutes a day. If we try to fit in our 15 minutes a day with the time we have left over, we will fail.

And the good news is ...

In the beginning, we may only have 15 minutes a day to build our business. But later, after we increase our income, we can dedicate more time in our day to our business.

It may be 15 minutes a day when we start, but it won't have to be 15 minutes a day forever.

SUCCESS REQUIRES THESE TWO THINGS.

Did we ever see someone work hard, and not succeed? Why does this happen?

Two factors are necessary for success. If one factor is missing, we fail. Before we go into aimless action, let's make sure we have these two factors in place. Working hard may be a virtue, but we want to work hard **and** get results.

Factor #1. A successful mindset.

We want our minds to work for us, not against us. Few of us had the privilege to receive a successful mindset from our parents. They didn't want us to suffer disappointment. So, they told us to be cautious, skeptical, and to lower our expectations. We end up setting low goals, or worse, no goals at all.

We may have tens of thousands of impressions in our minds that tell us we can't do something. It is hard to fight this overload of negativity. We need time to put positive impressions into our minds to counteract this huge storage of negativity.

Our journey requires a positive mindset. Prospects respond better when we have expectations for success.

There is a way to put positive impressions into our minds when we have only 15 minutes a day to build our business.

We'll visit that later on. For now, let's look at the second factor we will need for success.

Factor #2. A new set of skills for the network marketing profession.

No one expects us to know every skill of every profession in the universe. When we start a network marketing business, we won't have network marketing skills. The skills we have are for our current profession, not for network marketing. This means we must invest time and energy into learning the skills of our new profession.

Wanting something and having the skills to get it are two different things. Wishing, hoping, and pretending won't get results. We need to learn hard-core skills, such as how to move our message from our brains to the brains of our prospects. It takes skill to weave our message past the negativity and prejudices of our prospects. But we can learn how to do this.

Doing it right.

If we focus on a successful mindset, and a new set of skills, we will grow quickly. If we don't have these two factors in place, we will work hard … and fail.

Before we rush ahead into mindless hyperactivity, let's make sure we have these two success factors present in our lives.

Ready? We will start with our personal development time so that our minds work for us. We want our subconscious minds to work 24 hours a day, helping us believe that we will get to our destination.

POWER STRATEGY #1: CREATING MINDSET-LEARNING TIME.

When can we find the time to listen, read, and learn about mindsets and skills? And how can we do this while not using our precious 15 minutes a day? We want to use those precious minutes in personal engagement with people.

The solution is much easier than we think. Here are a few ways to put learning into our day.

#1. Using the first few minutes of our day.

In our book, *3 Easy Habits for Network Marketing: Automate Your MLM Success*, we describe this mini-habit that we can perform every morning.

Our alarm goes off. As we reach for our smartphone to press stop on our alarm, we immediately do a second thing. We press "play" on a personal development audio. This audio could be about our mindset, sponsoring skills, product information, or other things we need to know about our business.

We will play this audio in the background while we get ready for our day. Yes, in the background. It is not ideal but it's the best we can do. We don't have time to sit with a pen and notepad as we listen to this audio. We are busy people.

So while we shower, apply makeup, or make breakfast for the kids, we will listen and learn in the background. What happens in real life? We end up listening longer than a few minutes. This is bonus time for us to learn.

But our learning opportunities don't stop there.

#2. Using our commuting time.

If we drive to work, we can play audios in the car. If we don't drive to work, we can read and study on the bus or train. How much time do we spend commuting? We could spend much of this time reading, listening, and learning.

What do most people do during their commuting time? They waste it.

For some people, they listen to country music. Yes, they memorize the depressing lyrics. Definitely not a good use of time if they want to build a business. Other people relax, listen to elevator music, daydream, and look out the window. What are they dreaming about? They dream about what life would be like if they didn't have to go to their job. Dreaming is nice, but it won't get rid of that job. We have to take action.

Commuting time could be an hour or more every day. That is a lot of learning time.

#3. Using the time we spend on low-level activities.

Throughout our day, not every activity requires high-level rational thinking. Many activities we can do on autopilot. This leaves our mind free to learn personal development and networking skills. Here are a few of those times:

Mowing the grass.

Washing dishes.

Walking to the store or a neighbor's house.

Cleaning out the garage.

Cleaning the house.

Watching the children play in the park.

Exercising on the treadmill.

Make a list of these times. Then, plan to have some training material available for these minutes.

#4. What if we like to read instead?

If part of our daily routine is to read for 15 minutes before we sleep at night, all we have to do is change our reading material. Instead of an entertaining novel, we can choose to read a book on network marketing skills, or on having a positive mind.

What if our routine is reading the morning newspaper or scanning news on the Internet? Most news is negative. Positive news seldom makes the headlines. When we read negative news, we put more negative thoughts in our subconscious mind. Remember, our mission is to balance our accumulated negativity with more positive thoughts.

But we worry, "What will happen if we don't read the news?" Don't panic. If anything important happens, our friends will notify us. Negative news is a popular topic among friends.

Instead of our daily negative news, we fill these minutes with learning about positive skills and mindsets. Think of all the skills we could learn while others read the depressing news. We could learn communication skills, closing skills, prospecting skills, how to program our minds, and more.

POWER STRATEGY #2: CREATING LEARNING TIME FOR THE FOUR CORE SKILLS.

We now have our plan in place to improve our mindset. We can build our mindset in the background so that we don't waste any of our 15 minutes a day.

We want to spend our 15 minutes a day in action. That means talking to prospects, presenting, closing, and leading our team. Our 15 minutes a day must be focused, concentrated action. The following activities don't count as a focused, concentrated action:

Rearranging our diary.

Browsing social media to see what our friends are doing.

Cleaning up our desk.

Re-reading the company newsletter.

Chatting with our upline about new product rumors.

Choosing our clothes for tonight's meeting.

These are not business-building activities, and shouldn't be priorities.

Every one of our 15 minutes must be used on the most effective, efficient activities that will build our business.

Effective means we are doing the most valuable activity for the moment.

Efficient means we get results in the least amount of time.

When will we have the time to learn the core skills of our network marketing business?

We will use the same background time that we use for improving our mindset. We can listen or read during these off-peak times of our day.

Motivation is nice, but we need the skills to do the job.

And which skills should we learn in the background?

We know where we want to go, but we don't know how to get there. The most common strategy of new distributors is to hope, wish, pretend, and fake success in the hope that success will magically appear.

The problem? This doesn't work.

Yes, we may have the mindset and positive attitude. Unfortunately, what we are missing are the skills to make it happen. One of the most frustrating feelings is to want something badly, but lack the skills to make it happen.

As in any profession, there are core skills we need to learn. Dentists need skills. Engineers need skills. Accountants need skills.

Network marketing is no different.

What are some of the core basic skills we need to learn so that our dreams come true? Here are four core skills we should focus on in the beginning of our careers:

#1. Creating trust and belief in our prospects. If our prospects don't believe the good things we say, we have no chance. Our companies could offer the best plan in the world, but if there is no trust or belief, our prospects won't engage. Fortunately, this only takes a few seconds to do. But if we don't know how to create that trust or belief, we will lead frustrating careers.

#2. Learning creative ice breakers. We want to turn social conversations and chit-chat into conversations about our business. We don't want to look like greedy or sleazy salespeople. Instead, we want to guide people who have problems to consider our solutions. This removes that icky feeling that we have when we plead with people to look at our company video, or review our literature.

#3. How to close our prospects. We don't take closing lessons in school, and our parents didn't teach us this skill either. So, of course we can't understand how our prospects make decisions. What happens in our prospects' minds? How can we help our prospects overcome their fear of change if we don't know what is happening in their minds? We have to learn this new skill so that we are effective when we talk to people. When we don't use this skill, closing creates fear and rejection. That is a bad combination.

#4. Understanding when and how to give a presentation. Regrettably, we still give presentations like they were given in the 1960s. In the old days, salespeople were taught to talk **at** people, tell them to hold their questions until the end, and unload unlimited information in the hopes that this would convince prospects to buy or join. Modern brain science shows us that this is the perfect way to repel people. Yes, what we thought worked actually pushes people away. We need to learn the new methods of how to present.

The bottom line?

If we are not where we want to be in our network marketing business, it may not be our mindset that is holding us back. Jumping up and down at events, putting on a brave face, and thinking positive affirmations before we talk to prospects can only take us so far.

In most cases, we are missing the hard-core skills of how to engage prospects and get them to make decisions. Putting our efforts into learning these core skills may be the fastest way for us to reach our dreams.

Power Strategy #3: Decisive leadership.

It happens. A team member complains, "My business isn't working."

We know that businesses don't work. **We** work. But how do we avoid spending endless hours helping our team members with this problem?

The answer? We must quickly diagnose the real reason their business is not working.

Fortunately, this is very easy to do. There is a simple formula. All we have to do is ask ourselves this question:

"Does my team member fail in his business because he WON'T do it, or because he CAN'T do it?"

Now we know the right problem to address. We won't waste time.

1. If our team member fails because he WON'T do it, this is a mindset problem. More personal development is needed. Our team member has internal programs holding him back from action. Giving our team member more techniques won't solve the problem.

2. If our team member fails because he CAN'T do it, this is a skill problem. Now we should help our team member learn exactly what to say, and exactly what to do, when talking with prospects. More motivation won't help. No matter how

motivated we are, we still have to know how to do our job. One of the biggest frustrations for new team members is having the motivation, but not the skills to accomplish what they want.

As leaders, we want our team members to improve and move forward. By knowing exactly what is holding them back, we can point them in the right direction for immediate improvement.

Diagnosing this problem doesn't take much time. And, we won't spend endless hours consoling team members about their lack of progress. Instead, we move quickly to fix the problem.

All we have to do is remember this one question:

"Does my team member fail in his business because he WON'T do it, or because he CAN'T do it?"

POWER STRATEGY #4: GETTING PROSPECTS.

We need prospects fast. We can't wait for prospects to magically come to us.

Most people start with their warm market, people that they know. This is a quick and efficient way to get an audience. Why?

Prospects go through five mental steps to make their decisions. The first two steps are:

#1. Who are you? If we are a stranger, this will take a bit of time for our prospect to process.

#2. Can I trust you and believe you? This second mental step is very important. If we are talking to someone we know, we don't have to invest time to establish trust.

But I only know a few people.

Here is the good news. Most people are pre-sold as prospects for our opportunity.

Ask 100 people this question: "Do you want more money in your life or less money?"

What do you think they would say? "More money!"

If almost everyone is a prospect, that means we don't have to look for prospects. Looking for prospects takes a lot of time. Instead, we will learn to create pre-sold prospects on demand.

Creating prospects instantly means that we can prospect effectively anywhere, anytime. Even if we only have a few seconds, we can create new prospects.

Will this require learning some new skills? Yes.

So let's learn exactly what to say to create these brand-new prospects.

PROSPECTING SKILLS.

Only have 15 minutes a day? A big advantage is that we have to get to the point. We don't have time for idle chit-chat with others. Conversations about the weather, last night's big game, or the latest television show won't move our business forward. Our limited time means:

#1. We want to know if the people we talk to are interested or not.

#2. We want to talk to people who are ready to take action.

Many people will take months to make up their minds. Some have to wait until they have the perfect conditions in their lives. Some people are only curiosity-seekers. Can these people eventually become good prospects after constant nurturing? Yes, but this doesn't fit our current time schedule for building our business.

We can only concentrate on the prospects who can move forward now.

What are some of the questions or approaches we can use to gauge our prospect's initial interest? Here are some ideas.

"Are you married to your job, or are you open-minded?"

Talking to closed-minded people is a waste of time. We don't move our business forward, and we take time out of their day. Most people will say that they are open-minded, so we have to "read between the lines."

If their answer is skeptical or noncommittal, now is not a good time for us to talk. They may eventually become good prospects, but it will take a long time for them to take action. If we spend our limited time chit-chatting with them, we will miss good prospects who are ready to go to work now.

What kind of skeptical answers might we hear?

"Well, it depends on what it is."

"Well, I don't know. I am pretty busy."

"Of course I'm open-minded. But I don't want to get involved in any business or selling."

"Sure, I am open-minded. But after I finish work, I just want to relax."

Picking up a trend?

Yes, these people could be good prospects in the future. But now is not their best time to join. We want them to join when the time is right for them, not when the time is right for us. They will appreciate our empathy and understanding.

For now, we won't waste more of our valuable time. Instead, we will follow up with them from time to time. And who knows? Because we were gracious and not needy, when the time is right for them, they will call us.

They will call us?

Yes. If we plant enough seeds, some of the seeds will germinate and sprout on their own. They will contact us, wanting to move forward when the time is right for them.

A few years ago, I met someone at a personal development workshop. After the workshop, I explained briefly how our business worked. His response? "Too many changes going on in my life now."

Three years later, I got a phone call. The caller said, "Hello? Remember me? We chatted after that personal development seminar and you showed me your business. Well, now I am ready to start. I sorted out those messy situations in my life, got a job, and hate my job. Can you help me get started?"

My response? "Sure." One word.

If we plant enough seeds, this will happen over and over. When we are not pushy, our prospects will feel good about contacting us when the time is right for them. The worst thing we can do is push people outside of their comfort zones and force them to join. With our limited time, we want to allow our prospects to volunteer.

We can work with 1,000 volunteers. But ... we can only drag one unmotivated, limp body with us as we try to build our business. Working with volunteers is better.

"Are you looking to do something different, or are you okay staying where you are?"

We are looking for dissatisfaction.

If people are comfortable where they are, they won't have the motivation to change. To build a business, we need motivation and drive. We won't have a boss, so we have to push ourselves.

This question prompts people to think. They never noticed that they were in a rut. But once we bring this question up, they reconsider. They might think, "Hey, I don't have much patience for this job. It's boring. I would like to do something more interesting."

We planted a seed.

This person might ask, "What did you have in mind? Yes, I am interested in doing something different." This is the type of person we want to talk to now.

But what if this person is unsure? He says, "Oh, I don't know. Maybe. But I am pretty busy right now."

The good news is that we planted a seed. This seed can grow over weeks and months. But we don't have to stand there and watch the seed grow. We can be busy finding other people while this seed is growing. We want to spend our time with people that want to engage ... now.

An example of people who want to engage now?

While having a snack at a restaurant in Belgium with my friend, Jean-Phillipe Hulin, he asked the waiter, "Are you looking to do something different, or are you okay staying where you are?"

Immediately the waiter's eyes lit up and he answered, "Of course! I am working extra hours today on short notice." We told the waiter we would talk to him when he finished work for the day. Twice the waiter checked back with us to make sure we would be meeting him when he finished work. That qualifies as someone who is eager to engage ... now.

Look for people with two jobs.

People don't want two jobs. They already have a job; adding another one means no free time for them. No time for the family, no time for friends, no time for themselves.

But what do we know about these busy people? We know that they don't want to be this busy for the rest of their lives. Life was made for living, not just for working jobs during our waking hours.

People with two jobs have motivation. They want change. And they are willing to work hard to get what they want. Want proof? They have two jobs!

Busy people might use the objection, "I don't have time." But think about this. We can show them how to build their business in 15 minutes a day. They will have time.

What do you think these two-job prospects will hate most? Working two jobs for the rest of their lives? Or rearranging 15 minutes in their day so that they can build a business, a business that could help them eliminate one or even both of their jobs?

Most people would choose rearranging 15 minutes of their day to get out of their two-job lives.

What do we say to these people? "I know you are busy. But you probably don't want to work two jobs for the rest of your life. Can we talk for a few minutes to look at an option?"

We should gauge their reaction. If they are too guarded and skeptical, that could mean two things.

1. They don't trust us. (We will need to work on improving this skill.)

2. Now is not a good time for them. (Yes, they could have other stresses at this moment.)

If our prospect is curious and excited, that means we connected with him. We will enroll a new team member, and that person can look forward to at least one less job in the future.

As an added benefit, we feel good that we helped someone change their life.

Approaching people that we know.

We have rapport and trust with people that we already know. They have experience with us. However, we will feel guilty if these people think, "Oh, you are just trying to make money off of me."

Because we have this feeling, we are hesitant to approach everyone that we know. And, some people are intimidating. We have no idea how to approach them without rejection.

To solve this, we will use the comfortable/uncomfortable formula. This allows us to tell them we have an opportunity but gives them an escape so they don't feel trapped. Here it is in action.

"Mary, I am perfectly comfortable with your decision to look at my business or not. But I was uncomfortable not asking you if you wanted to look, and having you think that I didn't care."

How does Mary feel when she hears this invitation to hear about our business? She feels good. If she has an interest, she feels honored that we wanted to talk to her right away. If she doesn't have an interest, we told her that it is okay if she doesn't want to look. She doesn't feel bad. We didn't jeopardize our friendship. We don't feel guilty. And with this formula, we can approach everyone.

Let's do another example.

"John, I am listening to an online business presentation tonight. This is a business that you can do too. I am comfortable if you want to join me tonight, or not. No problem. I just felt uncomfortable not letting you know about this business."

How does John feel? Good. He has options. We don't judge him or our friendship based on which option he takes. All we did was offer him one additional choice for his life.

Another example?

"Hi, Linda. I got tired of working overtime at my job for extra money, so I started a part-time business from my home. I thought it would be interesting for you also. I am comfortable if you want to take a look at it, or not. I just felt uncomfortable not letting you know about it."

With this technique of comfortable/uncomfortable, we only take the volunteers.

The volunteers are ready for action. If we have to force or press for an appointment, what does that signal to us? Either our prospects are skeptical of our approach, or it is not the right time for them. Both situations will burn up a lot of our time. We can't afford that now. Later, we will have more time and can connect with them then. For now, we need to build our business fast with our limited time.

We like this comfortable/uncomfortable formula as it gets to the point quickly. We won't have people lingering on our "to call" list because we don't know what to say. It only takes a few minutes to sort out the people who are interested.

What happened to Dave.

Dave lived with fear. Yes, calling his friends, family, and co-workers caused Dave to have:

Heart palpitations.

Sweaty palms.

Nervous twitches.

Shifty eyes.

And a strong desire to watch television wrapped in a blanket.

Thinking about these calls turned Dave into a mess.

So what did Dave do? He practiced. Not with a "live" person, but he practiced with his bedroom mirror.

First, Dave practiced his comfortable/uncomfortable script for two minutes. That was enough stress for the first day. The second day, he felt better and practiced for three minutes. Not great progress, but still progress.

How long did it take for Dave to feel better about his script? Only three days. It was magic.

What happens when we practice in front of the mirror?

We make eye contact with ourselves.

When we smile, the mirror smiles back.

The mirror never judges us.

No worries about having to look at our notes.

After day three, Dave felt more confident. He asked his wife for constructive criticism. Dave felt safer with his wife's constructive criticism than to actually try the script himself.

Finally, after a few more days, Dave could say his script with confidence. We could sense this confidence in the tone of Dave's voice.

Total time to get over the fear of contacting his friends, relatives, and co-workers? Five days.

15 minutes a day can help us conquer our fears.

We can also overcome our procrastination.

Procrastination? Yes, we all put off tasks that are unfamiliar or scary. But small steps in a few minutes a day can change our career. We grow our confidence by moving forward one small step at a time.

We don't have to mentally prepare ourselves for a marathon. This is only a quick sprint. It takes less than 15 seconds to say the comfortable/uncomfortable script. These easy-to-say scripts keep rejection away. It is easier to be brave when we don't risk rejection.

So jump in and get it done. It is like ripping off a bandage. Don't hesitate. Just make the call with rejection-free words, and then it is over. We achieve our goal of today's call and we can move on with our day.

The more we practice, the better we get. Soon, this becomes easy and automatic.

What if we have more than 15 minutes?

Congratulations! If we have more than 15 minutes a day to commit to our business, then we should use that extra time. But be cautious. When we are not under a time restriction, it becomes easy to waste that extra time.

Having only 15 minutes a day keeps us focused. This forces us to use the most effective scripts and techniques.

Fear-buster mindset.

In Texas, we have a saying: "Dogs know who to bite." Pets can sense when we are friendly with a hidden agenda of taking them to the vet.

The subconscious mind picks up micro-expressions, the tone of voice, and subtle body language signals. This helps our prospects perceive someone's true intention. Yes, our prospects can sense our agenda. Here are some agendas our prospects might detect from us:

- I want to sell you my new product or service.
- I am friendly to you now so I can get an appointment for a presentation.
- I only need three more phone numbers from prospects to reach my goal today.
- This is a conditional friendship that ends if I can't get a presentation.

We might feel like we are hiding our intentions, but our intentions will show through.

However, there are other mindsets and intentions that we can have. Here are some examples:

- Most prospects want what we have to offer. They want good health, great skin, extra money, great services, and more.

- We do our prospects a favor by letting them know this is available.

- We offer this to our prospects as "one more option" in their lives.

Prospects appreciate extra options in their lives. Who wouldn't? We could offer our option by saying, "This is one more option for your life. You can take advantage of this option now, later, or never. But you will always have this extra option."

What happens? Our prospects sense our intention is to add one more option for their lives. This helps us avoid the skepticism and distrust that causes our prospects to hesitate.

More prospecting skills.

We must focus on simple, quick opening questions or statements. We need to qualify prospects immediately. Sure, everyone may become a prospect eventually, but not today. All we have is 15 minutes, so we want prospects who are ready for action. And how do we know if someone is ready for action? We ask them. And then we take the volunteers who want to act now.

And those who don't want to move forward immediately? We don't feel rejected. We understand that it is not their time. We accept that this moment might not be the perfect time for our prospects.

Here are some more qualifying openers to locate more prospects.

"May or may not be your cup of tea."

When I started network marketing, prospects rejected me over and over. Years later, someone taught me the phrase, "May or may not be your cup of tea."

This phrase prevents rejection, but it does more. It sorts our prospects immediately. I did not realize that benefit at the time, but looking back, it made a huge difference. Let's look at the phrase and how we would use it.

When introducing our business opportunity to a prospect, here is what we could say:

"Mr. Prospect, this business may or may not be your cup of tea. But are you open to looking at a part-time business that could add $500 a month to your family's budget?"

What are the benefits of this type of opening?

1. We give our prospects an "out" to our proposal. It is easy for prospects to say, "I am not interested." They don't feel pressured, and no one gets embarrassed.

2. When we say, "May or may not be your cup of tea," we let our prospects know that we are not going to try to sell them into a business. We will simply present, and they can decide for themselves. This removes fear from our prospects. This also brings down the wall of sales resistance.

3. This phrase signals to our prospects that we are offering one more option for their lives. Who wouldn't want extra options for their lives?

4. Curiosity will motivate many prospects to ask for more information.

5. If our prospects say "yes" to our proposition, what do we know about these prospects? First, these prospects are open-minded. Second, our prospects will actually listen, because they do not feel that we are selling or pressuring them. And third, we know we will have volunteers. We don't have time for skeptics. Only time for volunteers.

"Do you want to do something about it?"

Every day we have conversations. This is part of life. If we are good listeners, we can use some of this conversation time to build our business.

How? By listening for other people's problems. When other people talk, they love telling us about the problems and drama in their lives. Nobody wants to feel miserable alone.

But what do we know about other people's problems? We know that people want to solve their problems. Most people don't want to keep their problems.

If our business or product can solve our prospects' problems, we need to quickly find out if they want to fix their problems. How do we find out?

By asking the simple question, "Would you like to do something about it?"

All we have to do is listen for their answers. In a few seconds, we know if encouraging this conversation will be fruitful, or a waste of time.

Here is an example. After listening to an elderly lady complain about her ailments, I asked, "Do you want to do something about it?"

She answered, "Oh no. My children visit me much more when I pretend to be sick."

I remember my shock at her answer. I knew that it wasn't her time to fix her problem. She wanted to keep her problem as long as possible.

This saved me from investing more time trying to decide if she was ready for a solution.

A softer way to say this is, "Have you ever considered doing something about it?"

In-person conversations with prospects are better.

When we talk to people over the phone, we only hear the tone of their voices.

When we talk to people face-to-face, we hear the tone of their voices, observe their micro-expressions, and we also get to see their body language. Talking to people in person is a better way of communicating. Our prospects can participate in a two-way conversation.

But what about texting or messaging? Unfortunately, this is one-way communication. We are talking **at** people, not **with** people. We don't get the benefit of hearing their voices, understanding their intentions, or seeing their body language. Doing business through one-way communication limits our potential.

"But I only have 15 minutes a day."

We understand. Sometimes we only have time to send out a few texts or messages on social media. With our time limitation, we can only accomplish so much. If we must send a text or message, let's make sure we do the best we can.

If our intention is to get an appointment from our message, let's create a message that motivates prospects to call us. Here is an example of a very effective text that we can send.

"I've got a good story. I'll tell you when we have a chance to catch up and talk."

Here is why this text or message has a very high response rate.

#1. "I've got a good story."

The human mind cannot resist a story. We have to know what the story is. Then, we have to listen to the story all the way to the end, because we cannot go on in life until we know how the story ends. This guarantees that we speak to the curiosity program in the subconscious mind. Now our prospect wants to take action. Notice how we **don't** say, "I've got a good sales presentation." Prospects want to hear stories, not sales presentations.

#2. "I'll tell you when we have a chance to catch up and talk."

We don't want to continue texting or messaging with our prospect. We want a "live" conversation. Our prospect will request a phone call, call us, or offer to meet us for lunch the next day to hear our story.

At live workshops, we ask people to send out this message or a similar one. A high percentage of the participants will receive a text back requesting a conversation. It is that easy. And it is fun to do at a live event.

The next obvious question?

"What should I say in my story?"

Our story should accomplish the following:

#1. We should create instant rapport. We don't want our prospects to be skeptical. We need our prospects to trust and believe us so that our message gets through. To do this, we should use the words, "Well, you know how." This tells our prospects that they already know and believe what we are about to say next. This is also natural human conversation that doesn't set off any salesman alarms.

#2. Describe a problem that our prospects currently have. Naturally this will bring instant agreement. The purpose of business is to solve people's problems. Because our prospects want to solve their problems, they want us to continue the story.

#3. Next, we will announce that we have found a solution to the problem.

#4. It is decision time for our prospects. Our prospects normally say, "How does that work?" This tells us that their answer is "yes" to accepting our solution to the problem. That's right, our prospects make a mental "yes" decision even before they know what our solution is. From this point on, it is easy for us to provide a few details. Our prospects are pre-sold.

Here are a few examples of this technique. We will use "Well, you know how …" to introduce a known problem, and then complete a short story.

For opportunity.

"Well, you know how commuting to work takes a lot of time? I found out how we can work out of our home instead, and still earn a full-time income."

"Well, you know how things are getting more expensive every year? I found out how we can get an extra paycheck every month to help."

"Well, you know how we get all those credit card bills after the holidays? I found out how we can have extra money to pay all those bills."

"Well, you know how hard it is to get ahead financially with a job? I found out how we can get an extra paycheck so that we have money to invest in our future."

"Well, you know how jobs interfere with our week? I found out how we can have three-day weekends instead of two-day weekends."

For products and services.

"Well, you know how we hate putting chemicals inside our children's mouths twice a day when they brush their teeth? I found a natural toothpaste for children so that we will feel good every time they brush their teeth."

"Well, you know how hard it is to lose weight, especially after the holidays? I found out how we can start shaping up and lose weight in as little as nine days."

"Well, you know how sometimes we get stomach discomfort after eating spicy Indian food late at night? I found a special juice that helps soothe that burning feeling."

"Well, you know how we hate lying in bed at night listening to our skin wrinkle? I found a special moisturizing cream that prevents it."

"Well, you know how sometimes we feel tired in the afternoon? I found a natural energy drink that gives us energy all day long."

"Well, you know how growing old really hurts? I started a nutrition program that makes me feel like I am 16 years old all over again, but with better judgment."

"Well, you know how we get an electric bill every month? I found out how we can get our electricity for free."

"Well, you know how we don't have time to exercise and stay in shape? I found a healthy breakfast that we can eat every morning that helps."

"Well, you know how we don't like that chlorine taste in our water? I installed a portable water filter in my home, and now I don't have to buy bottled water anymore."

"Well, you know how we have to go shopping all the time? I found out how we can get extra cash back every time we shop."

Say better stuff, get better results.

If we must send a text or message, let's use the above examples to get an appointment for an in-person conversation. Trying to sell with one-way communications, texts and messages, is very, very difficult.

As we see in those examples, it is not difficult to get an appointment. The next step is to make sure our story and presentation is short, effective, and to the point. Nobody likes a long, rambling story.

PROSPECT AND CLOSE
IN SECONDS.

A few chapters ago we started talking about prospecting. We recognized our 15-minutes-a-day time restraint. What does this mean to us? It means:

#1. We want to know if the people we talk to are interested or not.

#2. We want to talk to people who are ready to take action.

Here is another way to check for interest and get action.

Tiny questions.

If you are not already familiar with the tiny question technique, here is how it works.

The only reason for business to exist is to solve people's problems. If people didn't need to travel, owning an airline would be silly. If we lived in the tropics, selling overcoats would be stupid. There is no reason for business to exist unless it can solve people's problems.

With this in mind, our first step is to check if people have a problem. This should be a small, noninvasive question. This helps us verify that our prospects have a problem that we can solve.

Here are some examples of tiny questions:

- "Do you find that things are expensive now?"
- "Do you hate commuting?"
- "Do you find that jobs interfere with our week?"
- "Don't want to work 45 years like your parents?"
- "Need more time off for the family?"

These are easy opening questions that shouldn't scare prospects.

But what about our products and services?

We can also create tiny questions about our products and services. Here are some examples:

- "Do you like taking good care of your skin?"
- "Do you find dieting hard?"
- "Do you like to travel?"
- "Do you get an electricity bill?"
- "Ever feel tired in the afternoon?"
- "Do you find makeup routines to be a hassle?"
- "Hate paying that expensive cellphone bill?"

Again, these questions are safe in most environments.

Now we know our prospects have an interest. Then what?

Our second question will close our prospects. We want to know right away if our prospects want to fix their problem now.

To get this commitment, we want to phrase our second question in the most positive light. So, we will start our second question with the proven word sequence, "Would it be okay if …?"

Here are some examples of using these words in a closing question. We will use the previous examples and show the two questions together:

◇◇◇

"Do you find things are expensive now?"

"Would it be okay if you had an extra paycheck to help?"

◇◇◇

"Do you hate commuting?"

"Would it be okay if you could work out of your home instead?"

◇◇◇

"Do you find that jobs interfere with our week?"

"Would it be okay if you had your own business so you could set your own hours?"

◇◇◇

"Don't want to work 45 years like your parents?"

"Would it be okay if you tried a different career path?"

◇◇◇

"Need more time off for the family?"

"Would it be okay if you had a part-time business so that you didn't have to go to that job?"

And for products and services?

"Do you like taking good care of your skin?"

"Would it be okay if you tried our new regimen for five days?"

◇◇◇

"Do you find dieting hard?"

"Would it be okay if you could lose weight one time, and keep it off forever?"

◇◇◇

"Do you like to travel?"

"Would it be okay if you could take luxury holidays for the price of a hotel room?"

◇◇◇

"Do you get an electricity bill?"

"Would it be okay if the bill was lower?"

◇◇◇

"Ever feel tired in the afternoon?"

"Would it be okay if you had energy all day long?"

◇◇◇

"Do you find makeup routines to be a hassle?"

"Would it be okay if you tried our four-minute system instead?"

◇◇◇

"Hate paying that expensive cellphone bill?"

"Would it be okay if your cellphone was free?"

Each pair of questions took less than 10 seconds. We found out if our prospects had a problem. Then we found out if they wanted to take action and fix their problem now.

Quick. Easy. And we could do this several times a day. Because this only takes a few seconds, we could fit this into the small gaps of time that we all have every day.

Can we improve this?

Yes. Instead of just talking about solving their problem, we can help them take action now. All we have to do is, after our first two sentences, suggest a next step.

What could that next step be?

- Opening an account.

- Enrolling in automatic ordering.

- Setting an appointment to go to the weekly meeting.

- Calling our sponsor.

- Asking for a complete presentation.

The next step is action. This is moving our business forward … now.

Here are some examples.

"Do you find things are expensive now?"

"Would it be okay if you had an extra paycheck to help?"

"Tonight, after work, I will come by and tell you the whole story. Two paychecks are much better than one."

"Do you hate commuting?"

"Would it be okay if you could work out of your home instead?"

"I will call my sponsor now and schedule a time when he can have a cup of coffee with us, and he'll show you his escape plan."

"Do you find that jobs interfere with our week?"

"Would it be okay if you had your own business so you could set your own hours?"

"Come with me to a business training tonight so we can get you started in your own business, where **you** set the hours."

"Don't want to work 45 years like your parents?"

"Would it be okay if you tried a different career path?"

"Come with me to our meeting tonight and see how many other people feel the same way."

"Need more time off for the family?"

"Would it be okay if you had a part-time business so that you didn't have to go to that job?"

"You can work the same part-time business that I have. I will help you make sure it works for you."

And for products and services?

"Do you like taking good care of your skin?"

"Would it be okay if you tried our new regimen for five days?"

"I will give it to you now if you promise to use it and tell me your results in five days."

"Do you find dieting hard?"

"Would it be okay if you could lose weight one time, and keep it off forever?"

"Grab your computer. We will get your healthy shake breakfast automatically delivered to you every month."

"Do you like to travel?"

"Would it be okay if you could take luxury holidays for the price of a hotel room?"

"Let's get online and get you registered as a smart traveler now."

"Do you get an electricity bill?"

"Would it be okay if the bill was lower?"

"Let's get you online now and make sure you get a less expensive rate."

◇◇◇

"Ever feel tired in the afternoon?"

"Would it be okay if you had energy all day long?"

"Let's order you a case of this natural energy booster, so you feel awesome all month long."

◇◇◇

"Do you find makeup routines to be a hassle?"

"Would it be okay if you tried our four-minute system instead?"

"I will show you how to use it online when you get home tonight."

◇◇◇

"Hate paying that expensive cellphone bill?"

"Would it be okay if your cellphone was free?"

"Let's take a break from work now and I will show you how it works."

◇◇◇

"But ... don't I have to give a long sales pitch first?"

No.

Prospects don't need facts and information to know if they want something. The facts and information come after they decide they want what we have to offer.

Here is our chance to be polite. Let's find out if they want what we have to offer, and if they want to take action on it. If they do, then we can chat about facts and information. But to chat about facts and information first is backwards. Our prospects will be wondering, "Why am I wasting time listening to this? I am not even sure if it is something I am interested in or want."

That is why we want our prospects to make a "yes" decision before the facts and information.

Remember, most of our prospects are pre-sold. They want the benefits of what we have to offer. For them, their only question is timing. The second question checks if the timing is right or not.

Timing?

Yes, timing. We don't want to be pushy or to put our agenda first.

Think of timing this way. Three or four times a day we are hungry. The other times? No. We are not hungry. Bad timing.

It only takes seconds to check if the timing is right or not for our prospects. We ask them, "Would it be okay if ..." and listen for the answer.

A FUN WAY TO BOND WITH NEW PROSPECTS.

Most people take a coffee break twice a day. But who made the rule that we must have our coffee break exclusively with our coworkers and friends?

Instead, let's think outside of the box. Our good friend, Amanda Maynard, created an idea called "Teavolution." What is Teavolution?

It is a virtual coffee break. We get a chance to video-chat with someone during our coffee break. This opens up many possibilities.

Meet someone on social media? We can deepen the relationship by inviting them to a virtual coffee break with us. For the next 15 minutes we can chat and build a better relationship.

This opens up a world of new potential friends, prospects, and eventually, team members. For example, imagine that we are in the skincare business. We can find potential virtual coffee break partners on social media in groups that discuss skincare.

If we represent travel services, we will find groups of travel enthusiasts.

How to Build Your Network Marketing Business in 15 Minutes a Day

Even better, we can find prospects who are entrepreneurs or want to be entrepreneurs. It is fun to have a virtual coffee break with people who have similar interests.

If we are like most people, we enjoy relaxing over coffee or tea. Now we have a chance to meet two new people daily at a deeper level. Because of the relaxed atmosphere, it is much easier to build a friendship.

This is one of many ways that we can squeeze more business time into our day.

"HERE IS THE SHORT STORY."

Long, detailed presentations? Not for us. We don't have time.

Before we invest time in detailed presentations, we want to make sure our prospects are eager to join. A simple way to do this is to give our prospects a summary before we start our regular presentation. How do we do that?

We say to our prospects, "Here is the short story." Then, we insert three or four of our best benefits. Now, we watch our prospects' reactions.

For some prospects, this will be all the presentation they need. For other prospects, they will start asking endless questions. In this case, we can schedule their question-and-answer session later when we have more time.

Want some examples of inserting our message into a short story?

"Here is the short story. Every month we get an electric bill. Now it can be smaller. Then we will have more money for movies and fun."

"Here is the short story. We can work a part-time job for the rest of our lives. Or, we can start a part-time business that can grow into a full-time income. Then, we don't have to show up for work anymore."

"Here is the short story. The desert air in our city can make our skin look like a prune. Our new moisturizer keeps moisture in our skin so it will look younger and healthier. Now we can keep wrinkles away an extra 15 years."

"Here is the short story. We waste two hours every day commuting back and forth to work. This costs us a lot of time. Our opportunity allows us to work out of our home. Now we can have more 'us' time and be happier."

"Here is the short story. You are careful about your health. You're already taking vitamins. These vitamins are even better."

"Here is the short story. All of your dieting, starving, eating funny foods, and exercising has got your body to where it is today. Invest in our product so that you can lose weight one time and keep it off forever."

Why does this work so well?

People love to buy. They hate to be sold.

Think about how people buy. Because they love buying so much, they buy stuff until they are broke. Then, they get credit cards so they can buy even more stuff. Buying is fun.

What do people hate? A salesman talking **at** them with a sales presentation. They want to get away.

Want to see an example of a salesman talking **at** us?

We go to a large department store to buy a big-screen television. The salesman says to us, "Shut up! Sit down. Let me tell you how wonderful our televisions are for the next 45 minutes. We won some awards. Our company founder was a genius at age three. Some famous people gave us testimonials. I have some videos for you to watch also. Hold your questions until the end as I might cover them in my presentation."

Is that how we like to buy? No. We hate this.

Here is how we like to buy. We go to that large department store to buy our big-screen television. All we want to know is how much the television costs, and if we can take it home with us today. We want the short story first. Then, if we feel a need, we can ask for more details.

If this is how we like to buy, why not offer the same experience to our prospects?

Why we should have a great short story.

This makes a better buying experience for our prospects. And, this technique is the antidote for negative prospects.

Imagine our negative prospect says, "I think this is a pyramid. I don't like you and I don't believe you. These things never work." Do we feel the negativity?

Our prospects often think, "I don't want to hear one of these long sales presentations. Let me think of any excuse possible to stop the conversation now. I don't care how good the benefit might be, I hate losing time to a long sales presentation."

Yes, most objections are requests by our prospects to avoid long sales presentations. But when we say, "Here's the short story," our prospects relax. They know this will take only a few seconds. This statement turns our negative prospects into listeners. And that is fair. We want our prospects to hear our message, and then decide if our message serves them or not.

Here are a few more short stories.

"Here is the short story. We love to travel and take holidays. Our travel business gives us the ability to travel at wholesale prices. Our new family vacations will be memorable. Plus, everyone likes to save money."

"Here is the short story. With our deluxe water filter, you don't have to carry bottled water home from the store. And with our finance plan, you actually save money because you don't have to buy bottled water again."

"Here is the short story. You and I are not getting any younger. Our retirement is getting closer. Our bank accounts cannot catch up fast enough. We need more money for our retirement. This is how we can do it."

"Here is the short story. Our children are only young once. We want to spend that precious time with them. We can't do that if we are at a job. With our business, we can work out of our homes and be with our children."

"Here is the short story. It is difficult to get rich while working a job. We need a business. You can start this business part-time, without risking your job. How does that sound?"

"Here is the short story. We want to help the environment, but we don't have time. Here is one way we can help. Simply change our toxic in-home cleaning products to these natural cleaning products."

Here is some more good news. Our short stories help our new team members immediately. In just a few minutes, they can share a short story to interest their initial prospects.

PRE-CONDITION OUR PROSPECTS.

We want our prospects to be aware of our products and opportunity before we present our solutions. Then we won't feel awkward when we bring our business into the conversation. But how do we pre-condition our prospects?

Using social media.

Posting pictures of our wonderful products from different angles? Yes, we know that is the wrong approach. Social media is for connecting. Humans love to talk and share their opinions. Let's give them a chance to share their opinion.

Imagine we share this on social media:

The four-question skincare test.

1. At what age does wrinkling most often begin?

2. What is the first area of the body to show wrinkles?

3. Can wrinkles be reversed?

4. Is warm or cold water best for cleaning one's face?

Now we gave our social connections a chance to share their opinions and participate in the conversation. Most will want to know the correct answers. Many will like to share their opinions. But what are they all thinking about?

Skincare. This is pre-conditioning our prospects before our conversation.

Pre-conditioning in face-to-face conversations.

In a previous chapter, we pre-conditioned our prospects by planting seeds. Our "planting seeds" statements and questions prompted many of our prospects to start an immediate conversation.

As a general rule, questions are better than statements. When we ask questions, our prospects can immediately participate in the conversation. People like to talk. We should give them that chance.

But there is another way to pre-condition our prospects. We can tell them our personal story, or the story of one of our satisfied customers or team members. Short stories will stick in our prospects' minds. Because stories are easy to remember, our next conversation with this prospect will be easier. Here is an example of a pre-conditioning story.

"I was a terrible sleeper. Some nights I would toss and turn and feel like a wreck the next day. Now I fall asleep within three minutes of my head touching my pillow. Mornings feel a lot better."

Whether our prospect instantly reacts or not, our prospect will remember this pre-conditioning story. And after a few restless nights, our prospect will remember us. Now when this prospect comes to us, this prospect is not only pre-conditioned, but likely pre-sold.

With only 15 minutes a day, we can't be inefficient with random conversation. Our prospecting time must include purposeful conversations and proven words.

A 15-MINUTE STRATEGY FOR FOLLOWING UP WITH PROSPECTS.

Do we have a fear of the telephone? Do any of these thoughts sound familiar?

- I don't know what to say.
- What if they ask a question I don't know the answer to?
- What if they are mean?
- What if I'm calling during their dinner?
- How do I start the conversation?
- If my first follow-up call goes bad, will I get discouraged?
- Are they truly interested?

And this fear gets worse.

When we do make calls to follow up with our prospects, what happens?

- No one answers.
- No one returns our calls.

Why does this happen?

If our phone rings, we might not answer because we are busy. We could be driving, working, eating, or not in the talking mood. Some people don't even recognize their own ringtone. And these days, most people would rather get a text.

Yes, the days of answering every phone call are history.

One fast solution.

If our fear paralyzes us, let's look at an easier solution.

Instead of making a telephone call, we will send a text or message. A text or message only takes a short time. Plus, there is no rejection. Follow-up does not have to take up large chunks of time in our lives.

The secret to a great follow-up message is what we say in our message. Here is an example of a great follow-up message.

"I know you are not interested, but if you know someone who hates commuting to work, could you please recommend me to them?"

This short message has three parts.

Part #1. The takeaway.

When we say, "I know you are not interested," this takes the pressure off our prospect. No more salesman alarm, no more skepticism and negativity. Our prospect feels relieved that we won't try to sell or push our solution.

When we take something away, many times people will want it more. This opening phrase sometimes motivates our prospect to think, "Hey, wait! I didn't say I was not interested.

And you know what, maybe I am interested. This opportunity you told me about might be perfect for me."

Everyone has this takeaway program in their minds.

When our mother told us, "You can't go in that room," which room did we desperately want to go into? Yes, we want what we can't have. It is part of human nature.

There is no chance of rejection when we start off with, "I know you are not interested."

Part #2. The benefit.

Prospects don't care what our product or service does. They only care about the benefits our product or service can give them. The second part of our message should remind them of the great benefits of our opportunity, product, or service. Here are some examples of the benefits of different products and services:

- Electricity: lower price.

- Diet products: losing weight without cooking special food ourselves.

- Skin care: to look younger, more radiant. To keep wrinkles away longer.

- Energy drink: feeling upbeat and positive all day long.

- Travel: five-star holidays for the price of an inexpensive hotel room.

Here are some examples of the benefits of our opportunity:

- Monthly income: This could mean paying for holiday gifts with cash instead of a credit card. Or paying off debt faster. Or possibly having enough money to fire the boss.

- Our own business: The benefits could include no more commuting, more time with the family, or setting our own hours.

- Win free trips: Much better than paying for our own holidays.

Part #3. Referrals.

Why ask for referrals? To save time.

Most people know at least 200 people. We don't want to talk to all 200 of their contacts. Many are not qualified, and most may not be ready to take action now. Out of 200 contacts, at least five contacts could be ready, willing, and able to move forward with our business immediately. We want to spend our time with them.

When we ask for referrals, our prospects mentally sort through their 200 contacts. Then, they can help point us toward the best possible prospects.

And it could turn out that the best prospects ... are the ones making the referrals! Yes, our prospects can change their minds after they see our benefits.

What is the worst-case scenario? We don't get any response or referrals.

What is a better scenario? We receive referrals.

What is the best scenario? Our original prospects tell us that they want to buy or join.

Putting it all together.

Remember our original message?

"I know you are not interested, but if you know someone who hates commuting to work, could you please recommend me to them?"

Do we see the three parts of our message clearly?

1. The takeaway.

2. The benefit.

3. Asking for referrals.

Now, let's construct some examples using this simple formula.

Electricity: "I know you are not interested, but if you know anyone that wants their electricity bill to be smaller, could you please recommend me?"

Diet shakes: "I know you are not interested, but do you know anyone that wants to lose weight without worrying about cooking breakfast? If you know anyone that might be interested, could you please recommend me?"

Skincare: "I know you are not interested, but if you know of someone that wants to reduce their wrinkles in a week, could you please recommend me?"

Body wraps: "I know you are not interested, but do you know anyone that wants to get rid of cellulite? If you do, could you please recommend me?"

Stress products: "I know you are not interested, but if you know someone who wants to reduce their stress naturally, could you please recommend me?"

Travel: "I know you are not interested, but if you know someone who wants to take five-star holidays for the price of a regular holiday, could you please tell them about me?"

Energy drinks: "I know you are not interested, but if you know anyone that wants to get rid of the afternoon yawns, could you please recommend me?"

Business opportunity: "I know you are not interested, but if you know anyone that wants to get rid of his job, could you please recommend me?" Or, "I know you are not interested, but if you know anyone that hates commuting, could you please tell him or her about me?" Or maybe, "I know you are not interested, but if you know anyone that wants an extra weekly paycheck, could you please recommend me?"

Car bonus: "I know you are not interested, but if you know anyone that wants to stop making car payments, could you please recommend me?"

Retirement income: "I know you are not interested, but if you know anyone that wants to double their pension in only nine months, could you please recommend me?" Or, "I know you are not interested, but if you know anyone who would like to retire up to five years earlier, would you ask them to contact me?"

New product: "I know you are not interested, but yesterday we introduced a new product that helps people sleep at night. If you know someone who has trouble sleeping, could you please recommend me?"

New incentive: "I know you are not interested, but we recently announced a new incentive where someone can earn $800 in their first 30 days. If you know anyone that could use the money, would you please tell them to contact me?"

Will we get a response right away?

Maybe, maybe not. We don't know if the timing is right for our prospect. But how long does it take to use this short follow-up script? Less than a minute. Yes, we can copy and paste this message and finish our follow-up responsibilities in minutes.

Here's one more way to reduce follow-up time with prospects.

Bob Paterson gives this advice: "Instead of selling, switch to solving."

Selling could mean presenting facts, showing videos, and telling our company's story. Lots of information to think about. But consider problem-solving. If we offer an option to solve our prospects' problems, the decision is easy. Our prospects can decide:

1. If they want to solve their problems by taking our option.

2. Or, if they want to continue on with their lives "as is" and keep their problems.

Bob says, "This problem-solving decision doesn't need 12 exposures and 20 follow-up calls."

Planting seeds.

It doesn't take long to plant a seed. But, it takes a long time to watch the seed grow. We don't have time to watch our seeds grow. However, we have time to plant seeds everywhere we go.

When we plant seeds, some grow, some hibernate, and some just die. With our limited time, we will concentrate only on those seeds that grow. This means we will plant the seeds today, but won't reap the harvest until much later. Once we know this process takes time, we won't be anxious and stare at our seeds for months.

Why we plant seeds.

Think about the average person we meet. Is this person in a frenzy and desperately looking for a business opportunity? No. More likely, this person is thinking about what to watch on television this evening.

It will take a bit of time to change this person's mindset. This won't be a one-time conversation.

Our 15-minute-a-day strategy will be to plant the seed of "wanting more" in one's life now, and let that seed grow. We can come back later, and our prospect will be thinking about a change in his life. Our prospect now welcomes our message with a more open mind.

The first step toward motivation is … dissatisfaction.

Not everyone we meet is ready to become our customer or start their own business.

If our prospects are satisfied with their current situations, our job is to help them want more. It is easy for prospects to get stuck in a rut. They end up doing the same things over and over as their lives slowly slip away.

If this is their intention, great. If this is not their intention, then planting a seed can help them change their lives.

But how do we get our prospects to acknowledge their dissatisfaction? How can we inspire our prospects to do something about their current dissatisfaction?

Easy. Use this question to start the process.

"Are you okay with …?"

One of our favorite questions is, "Are you okay with …?" This question gets prospects to think about the consequences of staying where they are. If they are unhappy where they are, this question prompts them to wake up and want to take action.

Want some examples of using this question in conversation?

"Are you okay with commuting and fighting traffic every day?"

"Are you okay with all the time the job takes from us every week?"

"Are you okay with how much money we have left at the end of the month after paying all of our bills?"

"Are you okay with only a few weeks of vacation every year?"

"Are you okay with having to ask the boss for a raise every year?"

"Are you okay with the time you have for your children?"

"Are you okay with working full-time until you are 67 years old?"

"Are you okay with your current salary?"

"Are you okay with taking your holidays at your mother-in-law's apartment with her 32 cats?" (Yes, slightly exaggerated.)

"Are you okay with making car payments every month, instead of having someone make them for you?"

"Are you okay with paying for your family holidays, when you could get these holidays free as a bonus?"

We don't have to limit this question to our business opportunity. We could use this opening question for our products, services, and other company benefits. Here are some examples.

"Are you okay with fighting your weight for the rest of your life?"

"Are you okay with fine lines and wrinkles forming before their time?"

"Are you okay with feeling tired every afternoon?"

"Are you okay with paying your entire electricity bill yourself, instead of getting a discount?"

"Are you okay with paying for overpriced skincare products that don't work?"

"Are you okay with shopping and not getting extra cash back?"

"Are you okay with feeling older than you should?"

Because this is a question, our prospects have to stop and think. Now they must make a decision to keep their lives the same, or to look for a change in their lives by taking advantage of our solution.

What is the common theme of asking these questions?

People make decisions first, and then learn the details. We have to get our prospect's "yes" decision **before** we waste time with endless details.

For example:

Let's say we want to get our driver's license. Do we know how to drive the car already? No. Do we know all the rules of the road yet? No.

The first decision we have to make is if we want to get our driver's license or not. Once we make that decision, then we can start learning the details.

Imagine that we want to become a doctor. Do we know how to operate yet? No. Do we know the side effects of the most common prescriptions? No. Have we filled out the application for medical school yet? No.

The first decision we have to make is if we want to become a doctor or not. Once we make a decision to go ahead with medical school, then we can start concentrating on all the details. We don't have to know everything before we register for medical school.

Here is one more example. Imagine that you invite me to a concert. All you want to know is if I want to go with you or not. If I start asking too many detailed questions, you would feel like it is a waste of time. For example, I ask:

"How much do the refreshments cost?"

"Tell me about the parking. Will we have to walk far?"

"Do you know who will be sitting close to us at the concert?"

Before you started answering these endless questions, you would want to know if I intended to go to the concert or not. It is the same in our network marketing business. With only 15 minutes to spend each day, we want to know our prospect's decision first.

People make decisions first, and then they can learn the details.

Now that we understand that people make decisions first, we won't waste time with endless details until we get that initial "yes" decision. We will focus our efforts on getting that initial decision.

What if we are talking to a prospect who insists on endless details first? In that case, we can turn the conversation back and focus on the initial decision by asking this question,

"Are you looking to start a business now? Or are you in the information-collecting stage?"

This simple question helps bring our prospect back to the big picture, the initial decision to want a business or not.

So let's plant some more prospecting seeds.

PLANT SEEDS EVERYWHERE.

Why everywhere? Because if we plant enough seeds, some will grow on their own. We won't have to spend time nurturing those seeds to maturity.

With only 15 minutes a day, we can plant a lot of seeds. Nurturing seeds takes time. That's time we don't have yet.

Let's look at some places to plant seeds now, so that later we will have a harvest.

Holiday parties.

What a great place to meet people. Holidays bring cheer and positive attitudes for the new year. During conversations with prospects, we could say this:

"This year was okay. I have plans to make next year much better. What about you?"

What will our prospects think?

If the timing is right for our prospects, our prospects will volunteer their interest by saying, "Yes, I want next year to be better also. Tell me about your plans."

This entire conversation took less than a minute. We now have interested prospects asking us for a presentation.

What are our options when our prospects ask us for more information? Let's list a few:

Set an appointment to meet later.

Arrange a three-way call with our sponsor.

Make an invitation to an opportunity meeting.

Send our prospects to a website.

Give a quick one-minute presentation.

Ask our prospects more questions to check their level of interest.

Give our prospects an information pack.

Yes, we have many options depending on the situation. The good news is that the hardest part is over. We located some prospects, and they are asking us for presentations.

In a conversation with a salesclerk or while checking out.

While chatting with the salesclerk, we casually say, "Getting by on only one paycheck is almost impossible today. I am still working on my plan. I hope you have a great plan."

What will the clerk will be thinking? "I don't have a plan. I need a plan. I better start thinking because my one paycheck does not go far enough."

The seed has been planted. Now we can check with the salesclerk from time to time to see how the seed is growing.

In a conversation with someone facing retirement.

Everyone eventually gets older. Retirement income is a concern for many people.

We can plant a seed by saying, "Retirement doesn't pay enough. So, I am working on a plan to double mine. By the way, what is your plan to increase your retirement?"

This forces our prospect to think, "Yeah, you're right. Retirement will come. I don't have a plan to increase my retirement income. Maybe I should ask you about your plan."

And now we have planted that seed.

Our prospect might ask us about our plan now, in the near future, or never. But if we plant enough seeds, some will grow.

Okay, now we know the technique. But let's go even further.

In the next chapter, we will take this technique to our jobs. We will illustrate how saying a few words now can plant our seeds, and sometimes even create prospects on demand.

COFFEE MACHINE CONVERSATIONS AT WORK.

Planting seeds is one of the most efficient things we can do with our limited time. If we plant enough seeds, many will mature into hot prospects with little or no more effort invested by us. We simply take the volunteers.

What do people do during coffee breaks at their jobs? They talk. And when people talk, they often complain. They mention the problems in their lives. And yes, some people have more problems than others.

Does every co-worker complain? Of course not. Some love their jobs. Their current career is what they always wanted to do. But these co-workers are in the minority. Most co-workers want more time with their family or less time commuting.

A simple statement during these conversations can plant seeds in the minds of our co-workers. We don't have to sell. We don't have to convince. And, there is no rejection because we are only making a statement. If our co-workers don't volunteer or respond, accept that the dream-sucking vampire boss has already turned them into human zombies, just waiting to die. Okay, a bit harsh and an over-exaggeration. But some people just exist and never think about taking action to do something different.

Here are some examples of statements that will make our co-workers think. The good news is that the longer they think, the more they will look for solutions to their problems.

Planting seeds of dissatisfaction.

"You know, we are not too old yet. Do you think we'll have a chance to do something more than this before we die?"

"Good thing our job is guaranteed. They guarantee us that we will never be rich working here."

"I can't see myself doing this forever. I am looking for an escape plan now. What about you?"

"This job has been a great start to my career, but I don't want to stop here. I plan to do a lot more. What about you?"

"If we work extra hard, our boss will get a bigger bonus. Want to hear my plan?"

"My dream in life is definitely bigger than this job. What about you?"

"If bosses earn more money, then why don't we become our own boss?"

"I was thinking this morning. Not much in my situation here at work is going to change, unless I do something about it. I have a plan now. What about you?"

"After working all month, and paying all my bills, I have $100 left. Tell me, do you think spending an entire month on this job is worth $100?"

"I am just curious. Which is more important to you? Money or the freedom to do what you want?"

"If we could set our own working hours, what hours would you set?"

"I thought to myself this morning, this job can't be my long-term plan. There has to be more to life. What do you think?"

"You know, nothing ruins a weekend more than Monday mornings. I wonder, what would we do with four-day weekends?"

"I am working overtime so I can make the payments on my car so that I can go to work. What about you?"

"Gas, car maintenance, car payments. It is costing me a fortune to come to work here. Soon I won't be able to afford it and will have to work out of my home."

"I don't think I want this job to be my entire life. I am going to do more. What about you?"

"This week looks exactly like last week, and the week before, and the week before. I can't see doing this for 1,000 more weeks of the same routine. I am going to make a change. What about you?"

"Just curious. If you didn't have to go to work here every day, what would you be doing?"

"I know we have a better future. We won't be here for the rest of our lives. Got any plans?"

"Every day I lose two hours of my life commuting to this job. Those hours are lost forever. How do you feel about losing those hours?"

"Did you look at our benefits here at work? We get an extra year of vacation for every ten years of employment. In about 500 years we won't even have to come to work! We will finally have time for ourselves."

"I hear most prison cells are larger than my cubicle. Only 21 more years until my release. How long are you in for?"

How are we doing so far?

Yes, planting these seeds is easy. No rejection. We wait for a few seeds to sprout and say, "Hey! Let's talk." It is fun when we talk to prospects who are ready for what we have to offer.

But can we be more creative? Certainly!

Let's create more statements and questions.

"When I applied for this job, I hoped and prayed that I would be hired. And now that I have this job? I am hoping and praying for a different job."

"I only see my kids for an hour every weekday. Thank goodness for weekends when I can spend some quality time with them."

"When I applied for this job, I was excited about a new career. Now that I am here, I think I will just settle for a paycheck. What about you?"

"You know, this coffee would taste a lot better at home. How about you? Does your coffee taste better on weekends too?"

"I tried to make a list of the reasons I love my job. Don't have any yet. Do you have some suggestions?"

"I love coffee breaks. I am thinking of a new career where I will have five coffee breaks a day talking with different people. Do you think I'm qualified?"

"These work hours are killing me. I am tired of using an alarm to start my day. What about you?"

"I saw people at the mall today during lunch. And ... they didn't have to go back to work at 1:00pm!!! What do you think they do?"

"Do we really want to do this forever? What else could we do?"

"My plan is to start a little business, earn enough money so that I will only have to work four-day weeks. Three-day weekends forever!"

"I know you don't want to work here the rest of your life either. So what are your plans to escape?"

"Staying here on our job until we die, and not changing anything, is a plan. I don't feel that it is a good plan for me. What about you?"

"I would love to delete the alarm clock app from my smartphone. What about you?"

"Our boss is a great motivator. He inspires me to improve myself and start my own business. What about you?"

"I have a new plan. I will let this paycheck pay for all my expenses. Then I will use my second paycheck for holidays and fun experiences for my family."

"Every morning I complain about going to work at this job. Then it occurred to me that if I don't like being here, maybe I should drive somewhere else in the morning."

"Our retirement plan won't be enough to live on. I am working on a plan to add to it. What about you?"

"If we are so smart, why does our boss make twice as much money as we do? Maybe it is better to be the boss of our own business. What do you think?"

"If we got paid twice as much, what would you do with the extra money?"

"I heard that a single cigarette shortens our life by two hours. Worse yet, a bottle of whiskey shortens our life by three hours. Know what is even worse? This job. Each day here shortens our lives by eight hours!"

"Any connection between this job and getting ahead financially is coincidental. It isn't working for me. What about you?"

"I saw my children briefly last week. They seem to be growing. What about you? See your children often?"

"When I graduated from school, this wasn't how I imagined my life. What about you? What did you dream about?"

"This job pays my bills. I'm going to start something part-time, so I can get ahead. What about you?"

"I think there is more to life than working 40 hours every week to make the boss rich. What do you think?"

"Do you think we will be 85 years old, standing here, drinking from the same dirty coffee cups? How long should we stay here?"

"I am thinking about giving up and resigning myself to work here until I die. Your thoughts?"

"Hey, let's work more overtime so our boss can get a big raise."

"We all would rather be at home instead of working here. What do you think we would have to do to make that happen?"

"We asked for this job, and we got it. Don't you think we should be asking for something else, or something more?"

"I spend one hour commuting to work, and another hour commuting home. That's ten hours a week out of my life! What would happen if we had careers working out of our homes?"

"I am thinking about starting a part-time business, so that I will only have to work here three days a week. What do you think?"

"Imagine what life would be with a five-day weekend instead of our normal two-day weekend."

"I want to retire early, and I have a plan. What is your plan for retiring early?"

"I had a dream last night where I worked out of my home. What do you think that dream means?"

"My family needs me and wants me at home. I have been thinking, who do I love more? My job or my family? What do you think I should do?"

"Do you think this job is the most important thing in our lives?"

Planting seeds, taking the volunteers.

Enough examples? Have we found at least a few that would be appropriate for the prospects in our market? Do we have a few opening statements that feel right for our personality?

With a little imagination, we could build a library of these seed-planting thought-provokers. The best thing about these statements and questions? It only takes about ten seconds to plant that seed.

Once the seeds are planted, we will let nature take its course. Many seeds will lie dormant and eventually die. But a few will grow and mature immediately during our conversation. These are the people we want to talk to during our limited 15 minutes a day!

Planting seeds is fun.

Once we focus on planting seeds, and stop worrying if each individual seed will grow, we will feel a sense of relief. We won't be attached to the outcome of each seed.

Prospects will notice that we aren't desperate. They notice that we only want volunteers when the timing is right for the volunteers. This makes us more attractive to prospects.

People want to associate with confident people. People distance themselves from people who think everyone has to join their business or buy from them.

But we are just getting started!

In the next chapter, we will create even more seed-planting questions and statements.

THE MORE SEEDS WE PLANT, THE BIGGER OUR HARVEST.

Why limit our questions and statements? The more options we have, the more people we can reach. Not everyone will respond to one benefit or problem.

The more tools that we have in our toolbox, the faster we can build our business. Here are more questions and statements that we can use in our allotted 15 minutes a day.

Let's think creatively!

More fun seed-planting statements and questions.

"My children asked me yesterday, 'If you hate your job so much, why do you go there so much?'"

"I was so discouraged yesterday. I thought about giving up and spending the rest of my life here. But today, I feel better. I am working on an escape plan."

"I have a plan. I will get an extra $500 from a part-time business, invest it in stocks, and then dump this job in 5 years. What do you think?"

"Where do you think you will be at this exact same time next year?"

"If we are still staring at each other 30 days from now, that means we haven't done anything to get ourselves out of this rut."

"We are in a rut. We don't want to do this until we die. What is your plan?"

"What would happen if we created a plan to get rid of this job and escape from here?"

"Looks like they want us to work 9 to 5 almost every day for the rest of our lives. What do you think of that plan?"

"Don't you think it is time that we became our own boss, instead of working for others?"

"So how old will you be when you finally retire? I was thinking we might be too old to enjoy our retirement then. What do you think?"

"So how much do you pay out of your pocket each week to get to work?"

"You know, I don't find great joy and satisfaction from my job here. But, I do enjoy the weekends. How do you feel?"

"Every day is the same. Alarm clock, traffic, job, traffic. I am ready to try something different. What about you?"

"I am curious. If we really, really hate this job, then why aren't we trying harder to find our escape?"

"I don't know about you, but I don't want to be here the rest of my life. I'm having coffee on Saturday with someone who left his job and started his own business. Obviously, he knows something we don't. Want to join me?"

"If you were paid what you were worth, how much do you think that would be?"

"My original plan of getting this job and becoming rich isn't working out the way I thought it would. What about you?"

"If you were paid what you were worth, what would you do with all that extra money?"

"If my part-time business continues to grow, I am thinking of cutting back to four days a week here."

"If I find a way to escape from this job, would you want to escape with me?"

"Do you feel like they are taking little bits of our brains out of our heads every day?"

"Isn't it a shame that coffee breaks are the best part of our day?"

Want some more examples?

"I am using this job as funding to start my own business. I hope to be out of here in less than a year. What plan are you working on?"

"Looks like the only way we can escape from this job is to die sooner."

"How is your retirement fund coming along? I gave up trying to save enough and am working on another plan."

"Only 30 more years of this boring work until retirement. Should we hang in there? What do you think?"

"I am collecting ideas on how to retire early. Got any?"

"If we are ever going to earn more money than our boss, then we can't stay here."

"This morning I figured out that I have 5,339 more days of sitting in traffic, waiting to get to work, and waiting to get home. I want to do something different with my life. What about you?"

"It is the start of a new year. I don't plan being here at the end of the year. What about you?"

"Well, here we are, stuck in the same place as last year. What are we going to do different next year so we don't end up here again?"

"How many more days do you think we should work here, before we do something to change our lives?"

"It is almost impossible to get by on one paycheck with today's prices. What are you doing for your extra check?"

"You know, there seems to be a lot of people who go shopping and golfing while we are stuck in this office. Who are those people?"

"You know, most airline pilots have part-time businesses. Wonder why?"

"Shouldn't we be doing something better with our lives instead of drinking this bad coffee and working, working, and working?"

"I woke up this morning thinking that I have 27 more years here before I can retire."

"I made a mistake. I thought this job would make me successful and I would have more money. What about you?"

"Wouldn't things be a lot more exciting if we were working in our own business?"

"What would your life be like if you sold your alarm clock to your neighbor, and could wake up in the morning any time you like?"

"Well, this job thing certainly isn't working out. Five days a week, and barely pays the bills. I need a new plan. What about you?"

"I feel psychic. I see us standing here, in the exact same place, one year from now … unless we do something about it."

"How much money do we have to make so we can pay zero taxes like the rich? I bet we have to have our own business."

"If we didn't have this job anchor around our necks, we could be home right now. What would you be doing now if you were at home?"

"Are you also tired of leaving home in the morning when it is dark, and returning home at night when it is dark?"

"What do you think the owner of this business knows that we don't know?"

"Bad coffee, bad job, bad pay. I can think of three reasons to start our own business. What about you?"

"There are two types of people in the world. Those that are open-minded and looking for opportunity, and those that are closed-minded and willing to accept whatever their boss will give them. I decided to join the open-minded group. What do you think?"

"I have some good news and some bad news. The bad news is that we work here. But the good news is that we can escape. What do you think?"

"Working here is slowly sucking the life out of us. You know, maybe you and I should start a business together."

"We all know that jobs won't make us rich. So what is your plan to beat the system?"

"I don't want to spend one more day here than I have to, so I have a plan. Do you want to hear it?"

"I spent 23 hours watching the Winter Olympics and didn't get paid for it. From now on, I am going to make a better decision on how to spend my time, so I do get paid for it."

"If you were your own boss, what hours would you choose to work?"

"You know, if we work really, really hard, and maybe do some overtime for free, do you think our boss will be able to get another raise?"

Still haven't found the perfect words for your co-workers? Let's do more.

"How long is our sentence here? When do we get time for us?"

"So how did you feel this morning when the alarm clock went off? Just think, we only have to do this 7,137 more times before we retire …"

THE MORE SEEDS WE PLANT, THE BIGGER OUR HARVEST.

"My part-time business bonus check this month was bigger than my year-end bonus here. I think I am going to take my part-time business more seriously now."

"I wonder who made the rule: 5 days for the boss, and only 2 days for us?"

"I might get a raise this year, or I might win the lottery. Same odds. How is your raise coming along?"

"We can stand here and complain about our jobs at every coffee break, but I have a new plan. Want to hear it?"

"Moving paper from one side of my desk to the other side of my desk isn't very fulfilling. If I have to work, I want a career with meaning. What about you?"

"You know, I would rather be sitting outside, enjoying the day at a nice sidewalk café ... instead of drinking this cheap coffee and going back to my job in 5 minutes. What about you?"

Enough?

Whew! And these are only examples for what we could say at work during coffee break.

Think of all the other places we could plant seeds. Here are a few:

Family reunions.

Class reunions.

Cookouts with friends.

Talking to retail clerks.

Visiting with friends.

Chatting with service personnel.

School functions for our children.

Sports events.

While traveling.

Standing in long lines.

Shopping trips.

The possibilities are endless.

We don't have time to do massive sponsoring campaigns. We can't chit-chat for months to build long-term relationships. We don't have time to do hours of cold calls. We only have 15 minutes a day. We barely have enough time to plant seeds and take the volunteers. But planting seeds takes almost no time out of our day. We can plant seeds anywhere we go.

That is the good news.

WE HAVE CHOICES.

Every day we get 1,440 minutes. Yes, that's a lot of minutes.

Will we choose to use 15 of those minutes to build a solid network marketing business?

The choices we make today will shape our results tomorrow. Consider what would happen if we chose to invest 15 minutes a day to:

- Reach out to one more person every day.
- Send one more private message every day.
- Pass out one lead generator.
- Ask one more person for a referral.
- Follow up with one person every day.
- Give out one more sample.
- Ask one more person a question.

These activities, over time, build strong network marketing businesses.

The shortcuts and strategies in this book can work for us … if we use them.

THANK YOU.

Thank you for purchasing and reading this book. I hope you found some ideas that will work for you.

Before you go, would it be okay if I asked a small favor? Would you take just one minute and leave a sentence or two reviewing this book online? Your review can help others choose what they will read next. It would be greatly appreciated by many fellow readers.

I travel the world 240+ days each year.
Let me know if you want me to stop in your
area and conduct a live Big Al training.

→ **BigAlSeminars.com** ←

FREE Big Al Training Audios

Magic Words for Prospecting

plus Free eBook and the Big Al Report!

→ **BigAlBooks.com/free** ←

MORE BIG AL BOOKS

BIGALBOOKS.COM

How to Meet New People Guidebook
Overcome Fear and Connect Now

Meeting new people is easy when we can read their minds. Discover how strangers automatically size us up in seconds, using three basic standards.

Why Are My Goals Not Working?
Color Personalities for Network Marketing Success

Setting goals that work for us is easy when we have guidelines and a checklist.

Closing for Network Marketing
Getting Prospects Across The Finish Line

Here are 46 years' worth of our best closes. All of these closes are kind and comfortable for prospects, and rejection-free for us.

Pre-Closing for Network Marketing
"Yes" Decisions Before The Presentation

Instead of selling to customers with facts, features and benefits, let's talk to prospects in a way they like. We can now get that "yes" decision first, so the rest of our presentation will be easy.

The One-Minute Presentation
Explain Your Network Marketing Business Like A Pro

Learn to make your business grow with this efficient, focused business presentation technique.

Retail Sales for Network Marketers
How to Get New Customers for Your MLM Business

Learn how to position your retail sales so people are happy to buy. Don't know where to find customers for your products and services? Learn how to market to people who want what you offer.

Getting "Yes" Decisions
What insurance agents and financial advisors can say to clients

In the new world of instant decisions, we need to master the words and phrases to successfully move our potential clients to lifelong clients. Easy … when we can read their minds and service their needs immediately.

3 Easy Habits For Network Marketing
Automate Your MLM Success

Use these habits to create a powerful stream of activity in your network marketing business.

Start SuperNetworking!
5 Simple Steps to Creating Your Own Personal Networking Group

Start your own personal networking group and have new, pre-sold customer and prospects come to you.

The Four Color Personalities for MLM
The Secret Language for Network Marketing

Learn the skill to quickly recognize the four personalities and how to use magic words to translate your message.

Ice Breakers!
How To Get Any Prospect To Beg You For A Presentation

Create unlimited Ice Breakers on-demand. Your distributors will no longer be afraid of prospecting, instead, they will love prospecting.

How To Get Instant Trust, Belief, Influence and Rapport!
13 Ways To Create Open Minds By Talking To The Subconscious Mind

Learn how the pros get instant rapport and cooperation with even the coldest prospects. The #1 skill every new distributor needs.

First Sentences for Network Marketing
How To Quickly Get Prospects On Your Side

Attract more prospects and give more presentations with great first sentences that work.

Motivation. Action. Results.
How Network Marketing Leaders Move Their Teams

Learn the motivational values and triggers our team members have, and learn to use them wisely. By balancing internal motivation and external motivation methods, we can be more effective motivators.

How To Build Network Marketing Leaders
Volume One: Step-By-Step Creation Of MLM Professionals

This book will give you the step-by-step activities to actually create leaders.

How To Build Network Marketing Leaders
Volume Two: Activities And Lessons For MLM Leaders

You will find many ways to change people's viewpoints,to change their beliefs, and to reprogram their actions.

The Complete Three-Book Network Marketing Leadership Series

Series includes: How To Build Network Marketing Leaders Volume One, How To Build Network Marketing Leaders Volume Two, and Motivation. Action. Results.

51 Ways and Places to Sponsor New Distributors
Discover Hot Prospects For Your Network Marketing Business

Learn the best places to find motivated people to build your team and your customer base.

How to Follow Up With Your Network Marketing Prospects
Turn Not Now Into Right Now!

Use the techniques in this book to move your prospects forward from "Not Now" to "Right Now!"

How To Prospect, Sell And Build Your Network Marketing Business With Stories

If you want to communicate effectively, add your stories to deliver your message.

26 Instant Marketing Ideas To Build Your Network Marketing Business

176 pages of amazing marketing lessons and case studies to get more prospects for your business immediately.

Big Al's MLM Sponsoring Magic
How To Build A Network Marketing Team Quickly

This book shows the beginner exactly what to do, exactly what to say, and does it through the eyes of a brand-new distributor.

Public Speaking Magic
Success and Confidence in the First 20 Seconds

By using any of the three major openings in this book, we can confidently start our speeches and presentations without fear.

Worthless Sponsor Jokes

Network Marketing Humor

Here is a collection of worthless sponsor jokes from 25 years of the "Big Al Report." Network marketing can be enjoyable, and we can have fun making jokes along the way.

How To Get Kids To Say Yes!

Using the Secret Four Color Languages to Get Kids to Listen

Turn discipline and frustration into instant cooperation. Kids love to say "yes" when they hear their own color-coded language.

ABOUT THE AUTHORS

Keith Schreiter has 20+ years of experience in network marketing and MLM. He shows network marketers how to use simple systems to build a stable and growing business.

So, do you need more prospects? Do you need your prospects to commit instead of stalling? Want to know how to engage and keep your group active? If these are the types of skills you would like to master, you will enjoy his "how-to" style.

Keith speaks and trains in the U.S., Canada, and Europe.

Tom "Big Al" Schreiter has 40+ years of experience in network marketing and MLM. As the author of the original "Big Al" training books in the late '70s, he has continued to speak in over 80 countries on using the exact words and phrases to get prospects to open up their minds and say "YES."

His passion is marketing ideas, marketing campaigns, and how to speak to the subconscious mind in simplified, practical ways. He is always looking for case studies of incredible marketing campaigns that give usable lessons.

As the author of numerous audio trainings, Tom is a favorite speaker at company conventions and regional events.

CPSIA information can be obtained
at www.ICGtesting.com
Printed in the USA
LVHW052341300820
664592LV00017B/2425